GREAT BRITISH STEAM TRAINS

A PICTORIAL HISTORY

MIRCO DE CET

AURA

Contents

Introduction

There is so much that we all just take for granted today. In our modern world of easy-to-drive automobiles, computers that give us instant news and access to information of all kinds, and comfortable homes that are stocked with all kinds of electronic gadgetry, we don't really need to worry too much, except perhaps about keeping our jobs and paying our bills.

Consider for a moment the world some 200 years ago when the United Kingdom went to war with the United States, Napoleon made his famous retreat from Moscow in 1812, the first photographs were taken in 1826, Queen Victoria ascended the throne in 1837 and the first postage stamp arrived in 1840.

These were all great events that helped to mould our world into what it is today, but possibly none was as important as the invention of the steam engine!

With the advent of steam came machinery that was far more precise and able to carry out intricate tasks at great speed. It was these machines of the 18th and 19th centuries that allowed craftsmen to harness their skills and work in a way not seen before. Initially, basic steam engines were used to remove excess water from mines in Cornwall. Then, as they progressed, they were used to mass-produce materials and goods in factories, but most important of all these were the first steps towards a new transportation system, the railways and the almighty smoking giants that would run on them.

The advent of steam changed the world forever!

The birth of the steam locomotive brought freedom to the public; they could now travel further and for longer. A day trip to the seaside at Brighton from London was now straightforward. Goods could also be transported to all corners of the United Kingdom.

Were you one of those little kids who grew up wanting to be a steam train driver? I know I was! Today, you can still have the pleasure and excitement of travelling on one of these incredible locomotives, thanks to volunteers and helpers all over the UK who turn out at weekends and holidays to set in motion these much-loved giants for our pleasure, and also to keep a little bit of the past with us.

1

Steam is the Dream

Innovators and Visionaries

The late 17th and early 18th centuries saw the emergence of steam as a major source of power and when it was finally made to work it changed people's lives forever.

One of the first people to be involved was a military engineer and inventor by the name of Thomas Savery [above], who was working on a steam engine that would pump water from the mines of Cornwall. These very deep mines would flood, causing all manner of problems – sometimes they would stop work altogether. One mine actually employed 500 horses to remove the water in horse gins and buckets; at great expense it should be understood! In 1698 Savery's engine [left] became the

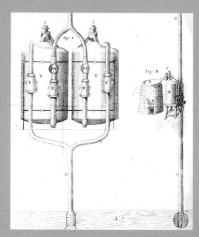

first commercially used steam-powered engine, but it was fairly primitive. Another Englishman, Thomas Newcomen, was an ironmonger in Dartmouth when he too became aware of the high costs of pumping water from the Cornish tin mines.

Along with his colleague and friend John Calley, he started experimenting with steam and came up with an atmospheric steam engine [right] in 1705. This was an improved version of the Savery design, but Newcomen was unable to patent his engine as Savery had obtained a broad patent for his pump in 1698. Newcomen and Savery then went into partnership and the first recorded Newcomen engine was erected near Dudley Castle in Staffordshire in 1712.

James Watt

A major player in the advancement of steam as a source of power was a Scotsman by the name of James Watt. Born in Greenock in 1736, he was the son of a merchant. When he was 19, he was sent to learn the trade of mathematical instrument-maker in Glasgow and, in 1757, he established his own instrument-making business.

In 1763 Watt was sent a Newcomen steam engine for repair and, while reassembling it, he realized that it could be improved. He understood that it would work more efficiently if the engine could cool the used steam in a condenser, separate from the main cylinder. What he needed now was financial help to back his idea. Initially, he contacted Scottish ironworks owner John Roebuck, but he went bankrupt, and so Watt had to look further afield.

The man who became his partner was Matthew Boulton, a successful businessman from Birmingham, and for the next 11 years they produced the Watt steam engine in quantity. At first, these engines were used to pump water from mines, but Watt continued to experiment.

In 1781 Watt designed a rotary-motion steam engine, which did a lot more than just pump water from mines.

By the time Watt had added all manner of adjustments and modifications, his steam engine could be used to drive a variety of machines, and by 1800 there were over 500 of these steam engines working in Britain's mines and factories.

Watt had previously been granted a patent by Parliament for his engine design, which stopped anybody else from making a steam engine like the one he had developed. For the next 25 years, the Boulton & Watt Company had a virtual monopoly over the production of steam engines and Watt was able to charge his customers a premium for using the ones he had made.

A model of the first fully developed Watt rotative engine.

Richard Trevithick

Richard Trevithick was born in Cornwall and from an early age was involved with mining and engineering; Cornwall was a hub for the mining industry. He became an inventor and pioneer of steam-powered road and rail transportation. His contribution included the development of the first high-pressure steam engine and he went on to build the first full-scale working railway steam locomotive.

The world's first locomotive-hauled railway journey took place on 21 February 1804 and it was Trevithick's unnamed steam locomotive that hauled the train along the tramway at the Pen-y-Darren Ironworks in Merthyr Tydfil to the bottom of Abercynnon Valley, a journey of roughly nine miles. The locomotive was loaded up with ten tons of iron, 70 men and five extra wagons. It completed the distance in about two hours.

Trevithick also erected a circular railway track in Euston Square, London. Initially seen as an exhibition of 'things to come', it turned out to be more of a funfair attraction. He charged the public one shilling – a fee that few could afford at that time – to ride on his latest steam engine named *Catch Me Who Can*. Sadly, it never caught the public imagination and soon closed down.

Richard Trevithick was the first British engineer to use what was called 'strong steam' – steam at very high pressure. But with this, there was always the fear and risk of a boiler exploding, which could cause damage and even death. It was unfortunate that, in 1803, one of Trevithick's stationary pumping engines at Greenwich exploded and killed four men. Trevithick viewed the accident as the result of careless operation rather than being due to any design defect. All the same, because of the danger, there was criticism of his design and James Watt even went as far as to say that Trevithick 'deserved to be hanged'.

Trevithick's engines [see right], though, were versatile and could be made in different sizes.

Smaller models could be manufactured with the same power output, and larger examples could be made even more powerful. Initially, though, they were far less economical to run, although their versatility opened up opportunities because they could be adapted more easily for railways, ships and agricultural usage.

Wagonways

Tracked roadways date back some 2,000 years and were used by the Greeks, as has been discovered with the 'Diolkos' tracked pathway near Corinth. Simple tracks were cut into the stone to help transport materials to and fro, but also to move ships from one section of water to another.

Wagonways (originally spelt 'waggonways' in the North East) at first used wooden rails, following the same kind of idea, and were created to

help transport coal from a minehead to a waiting barge or boat on the local canal or river. At this time, waterways, such as canals and rivers, were the best way of transporting materials between their source and their final destination, which could be a factory or just a collection area.

A horse would be used to move the wagon from the mine down to the barge or boat, where it would be emptied. Because of the steep inclines that could be encountered, the horse would often be tethered to the rear of the wagon to stop it from running away down the slope. On flat terrain, the horse would just pull the loaded wagon to the waiting barge or boat, where it would be emptied of its contents and then pulled back to the mine to collect the next load.

Wheel brake on a wooden wagonway wagon.

Although this sounds slow and tedious today, these wagonways improved the transportation of coal and could increase the amount being delivered fourfold. It seems possible that the original wagonway was used by James Clifford to transport coal from his mines in Broseley down to the nearby River Severn in Shropshire. What is certain is that the company, Huntingdon Beaumont, completed the Wollaton wagonway in 1604; it transported coal from mines in Strelley to Wollaston Lane End, near Nottingham. Fragments of tracks used at Mines Royal at Caldbeck – a mining monopoly of the period in the Lake District – have also been found. More recently in 2013, wooden rails were unearthed at the dig carried out at the Neptune shipyard on the estuary just outside Newcastle upon Tyne. These are now being preserved and treated at a local museum.

Choldron Coal Wagon

Shown here is a Choldron Coal Wagon, built around 1870. The marking '189' on the side refers to its stock number and the '2.18.2' to its weight: 2 tons, 18 hundredweights and 2 stones. This was subtracted when the wagons were weighed full. The 'L' stands for Londonderry: the railway was owned by Lord Londonderry who was a major coal owner in County Durham and lived at Wynyard Hall, near Seaham.

Hay Inclined Plane

The rails of the Hay Inclined Plane are still in place along the River Severn, just up from Ironbridge in Coalport, Shropshire. This site was dismantled when it fell into disrepair, but was later restored in the late-1960s. This system – worked by a combination of steam and gravity – was used between 1792 and 1894 to transport materials via tub boats. These were oblong-shaped cargo boats that could be moved up and down the inclined plane via wheeled cradles, from an upper water system to a lower one – in this case, from the Shropshire canal running from Blists Hill, at the higher level, to the canal basin at Coalport at the lower level. The Shropshire canal boats were box-shaped, 20 feet long and could carry five tons of material.

Tanfield Railway

The oldest railway in the world

Like many others, the Tanfield wagonway was used for transporting coal from the collieries in the County Durham area to the River Tyne. From here, colliers (ships that carried coal in bulk) would then transport the coal along the River Tyne to its destination. The oldest part of the railway, which is still used today, dates back to 1725 and, therefore, is considered to be the oldest railway in the world.

This historic wagonway started life with wooden rails and wooden wagons which had wooden wheels. They were drawn along by horses. Conversion to steel rails started in 1837, and by 1881 the line started running steam engines.

Causey Archway

The oldest single-arch railway bridge in the world

Causey Archway is the oldest surviving single-arch railway bridge in the world; it was part of the old Tanfield line that the horse-drawn wagons had to go over to reach the colliers on the River Tyne. It was built between 1725 and 1726 at the then massive cost of £12,000 and, when finished, it was the longest single-span bridge in the country with an arch span of 102 feet.

Across the top of the arch there were two rails: one, 'Main Way', took the coal to the waiting ships on the River Tyne; the other, 'Bye Way', was used for returning the empty wagons. More than 900 horse-drawn wagons would cross the arch every day using the Tanfield wagonway.

Matthew Murray

Matthew Murray designed the world's first commercially successful steam locomotive in 1812, which worked at the Middleton Colliery Railway and ran on cast-iron rails. *Salamanca*, as it was known, had two cylinders and was named after the Duke of Wellington's victory at the battle of Salamanca.

Salamanca was the first locomotive to use a rack-and-pinion system, a design created by John Blenkinsop. Four of these engines were built to work on the railway, but sadly *Salamanca* was destroyed six years later after its boiler exploded.

'The Collier' by R and D Havell (1813): in the background is a Blenkinsop and Murray locomotive on its way from Middleton colliery.

Puffing Billy

In 1812 William Hedley was commissioned by Christopher Blackett, owner of the Wylam colliery, to design a steam engine that could be used at their mine. The locomotive took the name *Puffing Billy* and was driven by a single crank on one side of the vehicle.

The Stockton and Darlington Railway

By 1820 men like Timothy Hackworth, George Stephenson and William Hedley, who all worked in collieries, had designed and built locomotives. Wagons, and in particular rail technology, were now advanced and these huge steaming machines were used to their limit transporting goods to ports and canals.

Working model of Stephenson's Locomotion No. 1 on display at the Darlington Railway Centre and Museum.

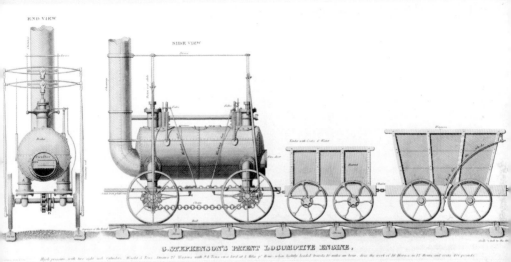

All the advances that had been made were now put to the test when the first steam railway was planned and built. This first railway was designed so that businessmen could transport their goods from the mines in County Durham to the port of Stockton on the River Tees.

After much discussion about where the line would go, the difficulties of avoiding people's private land and the type of vehicles that would travel on the line, one person was chosen to be the chief engineer of the project. That person was George Stephenson, who was assisted by his son Robert.

Finally, a new bill was presented to Parliament, requesting Stephenson's deviations from the original route and the use of 'loco-motives or moveable engines', which received assent on 23 May 1823.

The route was by no means straightforward and included embankments up to 48 feet high, a wrought-iron girder bridge to cross the River Gaunless, designed by Stephenson, and a stone bridge over the River Skerne which was designed by the Durham architect Ignatius Bonomi.

In 1823 Robert Stephenson and Company opened their locomotive works at Forth Street, Newcastle, and the following year the S&DR (Stockton and Darlington Railway) ordered two steam locomotives and two stationary engines. With the two stationary engines in place, the first of the locomotives was presented. On 16 September 1925 *Locomotion No 1* left the works and the following

*Crowds gather at the opening of the Stockton
and Darlington Railway in 1825.*

day an advertisement appeared in newspapers telling the public that
the railway would open on 27 September 1825.

When the opening day came, thousands gathered to watch as the
train, carriages and passengers assembled. The train set off and, with
a couple of unscheduled stops for repairs and maintenance along the
way, it finally came to a halt at the Darlington branch junction where
it was greeted by 10,000 people.

The locomotive then left for Stockton, now hauling 31 vehicles with
550 passengers. The train arrived to great fanfare 3 hours, 7 minutes
after leaving Darlington. The day was deemed a tremendous success!

The Liverpool and Manchester Railway

Liverpool and Manchester in particular became important hubs for the transportation of goods. Roads and canals served both cities, with Liverpool the main entry point for important materials from abroad, in particular from America.

The Mersey and Irwell Navigation and the Bridgewater Canal were then the prime means of transportation, but it was felt that they were making excessive profits from existing trade. The alternative was a railway connection between the two cities.

A second Bill of Parliament received the Royal Assent in 1826 but for quite a different alignment. The 35 miles of line were an incredible piece of engineering: there was the 2,250-yard-long Wapping Tunnel, which ran

A train crossing the Bridgewater Canal at Patricroft during the 1830s.

The Sankey viaduct.

underneath Liverpool; then came the two-mile-long cutting which was up to 70 feet deep at Olive Mount, the 70-foot-high, nine-arch viaduct over the Sankey Brook valley and the famous 4¾ miles crossing of Chat Moss. Sixty-four bridges and viaducts, all but one built of bricks or masonry, were also erected.

The line opened on 15 September 1830 with termini at Manchester Liverpool Road and Liverpool Crown Street. There were huge celebrations for the opening, but these were sadly marred by the death of William Huskisson, Member of Parliament for Liverpool. Huskisson became the world's first widely reported railway casualty after being run over and fatally wounded by George Stephenson's *Rocket*.

The Rainhill Trials

When the Manchester to Liverpool Railway line was nearing completion, the directors decided to hold a competition to see if stationary steam engines or locomotives should be used to pull the trains.

And so the Rainhill Trials, as they were known, were arranged for 6 October 1829; the ultimate winner would collect a prize of £500. Three notable names from the world of engineering were selected as judges and two or three locomotives took part per day. During these runs, the locomotives were to be tested for various abilities over several days.

Although ten locomotives were entered, only five of them actually began the tests: *Cycloped*,

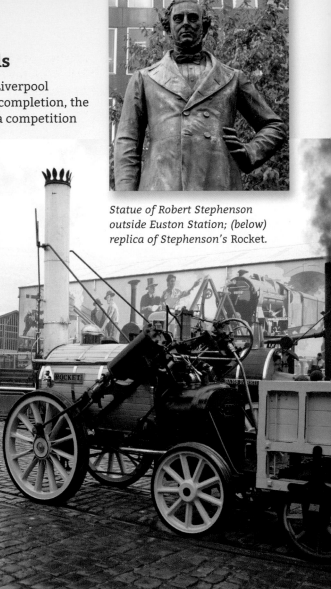

Statue of Robert Stephenson outside Euston Station; (below) replica of Stephenson's Rocket.

built by Thomas Shaw Brandreth; *Novelty*, built by John Ericsson and John Braithwaite; *Perseverance*, built by Timothy Burstall; *Rocket*, built by Robert Stephenson and Company; and *Sans Pareil*, built by Timothy Hackworth.

Cycloped was the first to drop out of the competition; next to retire was *Perseverance*. *Sans Pareil* failed to finish the trials and the last to drop out was *Novelty*. In this way, Stephenson's *Rocket* became not only the winner but also the only locomotive to complete the trials.

Replica of the engine Sans Pareil
(meaning 'without equal') and carriage.

Ffestiniog Railway

The Ffestiniog Railway was inaugurated on 23 May 1832 by an Act of Parliament. The route initially allowed loaded slate trains to make their way down the mountain by gravity and then to be pulled up again by horses. The 23.5-inch gauge was the same as that used in the quarries and worked well for both the horses and the wagons going up and down the difficult terrain.

As slate traffic increased, the gravity system and the situation with the horses came under review and thoughts turned to the steam engine. Due to certain restrictions though, one of which was the gauge size, the use of passenger traffic on a gauge that was less than the British standard gauge was not allowed.

Progress was only made after Charles Easton Spooner took over the railway

Merddin Emrys, *built for the Ffestiniog Railway in 1879 to the design of Percival Spooner and incorporating Fairlie's patent articulated 0-4-4-0 locomotive design.*

in 1856. He studied railway design and manufacture, and in 1863 contracts were signed for four small locomotives. These were transported by horse and cart to Port Madoc, entering service that same year. Just one year later, the Board of Trade gave permission for passenger trains to run, and so it became the first small-gauge railway to run passenger trains.

As passenger freight increased, new and more powerful engines were needed. But they had to be able to tackle the steep inclines and, in particular, the tight corners. Enter Robert Fairlie, who had designed a locomotive that could pull longer trains and, therefore, carry more passengers. The conclusion to all this was a double-bogie engine which looked like two engines that had been built back to back.

The first improved Fairlie engine – *James Spooner* – was introduced in 1872, followed by two further engines – *Merddin Emrys* in 1879 and *Livingston Thompson* in 1886.

In 1979 the Ffestiniog Railway was looking for a new large engine; it again chose a Fairlie double-bogie design and called it the *Earl of Merioneth*.

2

All Steamed Up

With the opening of the Stockton & Darlington Railway, people could see the benefits this type of transportation could bring, not only for goods but for passengers too, and suddenly the railway had arrived!

By 1830 nearly 100 new locomotives had been built, using both vertical and inclined cylinders. But things were moving forward at quite a pace and, while George Stephenson set about organizing the railway network, his son Robert was looking at new ideas and new locomotive engine designs.

Robert introduced the 2-2-0 Planet class locomotive in 1830, which would became the blueprint for all future locomotive layouts. Much had been learned from the Rainhill Trials and, even though *Rocket* had won the competition, there were still plenty of problems to iron out, in particular the pitching and rolling at high speed, which was caused by the cylinders.

Robert Stephenson carried out various changes to *Rocket*, resolving many of the problems, but the most significant was the relocation of the cylinders to the front of the vehicle between the wheels.

All these changes and more were introduced into the newly designed locomotive, *Planet*, and when introduced in 1830, it became the world's first mainline locomotive type. And so in less than three years Robert Stephenson had transformed the simple, coal-transporting locomotive into a mainline, Planet-class locomotive.

Timothy Hackworth

The Stephensons were not the only people delving into new designs; others too were hard at work designing new, and modifying older, locomotives. Timothy Hackworth, who had designed *Sans Pareil* for the Rainhill Trials, had taken on responsibility for Stephenson's *Locomotion* engine after the boiler had exploded and killed a worker. He improved the performance of the engine, but in 1827 he also introduced a new locomotive by the name of *Royal George*. The engine was mounted on six wheels with the cylinders in a vertical position on the outside of the boiler, while the pistons and connecting rods drove the rear wheels.

The Planet class was Stephenson's next major design change after *Rocket* and was the ninth locomotive built for the Liverpool & Manchester Railway. The locomotive was the first to use inside cylinders and had a steam dome added to prevent water from reaching the cylinders.

On 23 November 1830 *No.9 Planet* ran the line from Liverpool to Manchester – some 32 miles – in just one hour. Speeds were now increasing rapidly as locomotive technology advanced.

Robert Stephenson & Co. built a further six examples and three more were supplied by Murray & Wood in Leeds after Stephenson had passed on the design drawings for them to follow. The Planet, along with the Patentee class locomotives (built some three years later), was the first to be made in large numbers.

Patentee type locomotive

In 1833 Robert Stephenson & Co. introduced the revolutionary Patentee type locomotive, a larger version of the 2-2-0 Planet type, this time using a 2-2-2 wheel configuration. This system had two leading wheels on one axle, two powered driving wheels on one axle and two trailing wheels on one axle, giving the vehicle better stability and the ability to have a larger firebox than its predecessors.

The first train to run in Germany in 1835 was the *Adler* locomotive, which was a Patentee type. This completed a journey from Nuremberg to Fürth and was driven by William Wilson, a Scotsman, employed for the demonstration! Many other countries also bought the Patentee locomotive, and by 1838 this type of engine had become the standard passenger design.

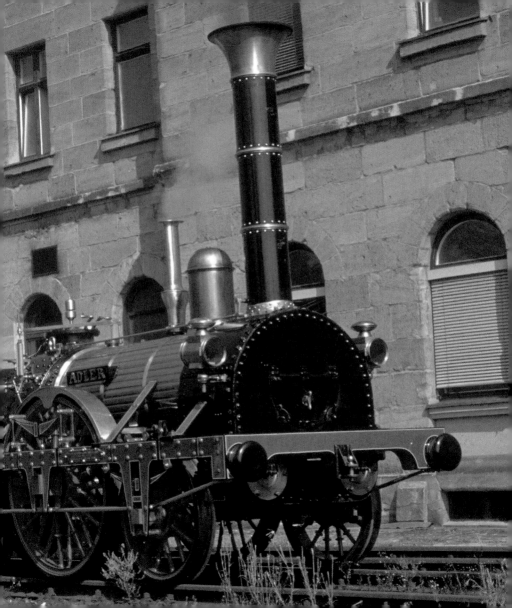

Lion

The Liverpool & Manchester Railway ordered two locomotives to haul luggage trains. These were delivered in 1838 and acquired the names *Lion* and *Tiger*. These were the first locomotives to be built by Todd, Kitson & Laird in Leeds. These engines used a conventional 0-4-2 wheel arrangement and had inside cylinders.

Lion has a particularly interesting story and it is only thanks to members of the Liverpool Engineering Society that it is with us today. In 1859 *Lion* was sold to the Mersey Docks and Harbour Board and installed as a stationary pumping engine at Princes Dock. It was here that it was spotted by enthusiasts and rescued for preservation.

Lion was restored at the Crewe Railway Works and was able to attend the 1930 centenary celebrations of the Liverpool & Manchester Railway. Before World War Two, it stood on a plinth in Lime Street station, but it was removed in 1941.

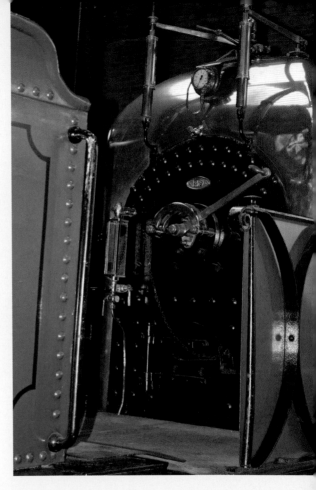

BRUSH WITH FAME

Lion has appeared in three films, *Victoria the Great* (1937), *The Lady with the Lamp* (1951) and *The Titchfield Thunderbolt* (1952).

'Long boiler'

As more railway tracks were laid, so the engines were able to travel further and faster. There was a need for more power and speed. The extra distances now being travelled by some engines were creating problems for the fireboxes and chimneys.

In co-operation with the North Midland Railway at the Derby Works, Stephenson measured the temperature of the exhaust gasses and came to the conclusion that a longer boiler would be the solution for future designs.

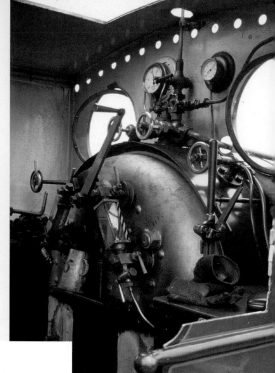

The first of these 'long boiler' engines were 2-2-2 design, but Stephenson moved the trailing wheels to the front in a 4-2-0 formation in 1844, which allowed the cylinders to be mounted between the supporting wheels.

Shown here is the Kitson A. No. 5 pannier tank engine built by Kitson & Co. to the Stephenson 'long boiler' design. It was built for the Consett Iron and Steel Company and has a cylinder size of 17 x 26 inches, with a boiler diameter of 4 feet and a working pressure of 140psi.

Isambard Kingdom Brunel

Isambard Kingdom Brunel, whose name comes from an amalgamation of his parents' names, was an English mechanical and civil engineer who is considered 'one of the most ingenious and prolific figures in engineering history'; he was a giant in his field and a prominent contributor to the Industrial Revolution.

Brunel built dockyards, the Great Western Railway, a series of steamships, including the first propeller-driven transatlantic steamship, and a series of important bridges and tunnels. His designs revolutionized public transport and modern engineering.

His railway designs were well built, minimizing gradients and bends, but because of this they were expensive projects. New bridges and viaducts were constructed, usually at great expense; the two-mile long Box Tunnel near Bath is just one example.

Brunel was convinced that a larger gauge rail system would lead to more comfort. 'Broad gauge' as it became known was just over 7 feet wide, in contrast to the 'standard gauge' of 4 feet, 8½ inches. Most engine designers at the time had been using the standard gauge, and naturally this caused massive problems when the two gauges met.

At the age of 27, he was appointed chief engineer of the Great Western Railway (GWR) and it was his work on this railway, starting in 1833, that established him as one of the world's leading engineers. The line from London to Bristol took in some impressive achievements, like the viaducts at Hanwell and Chippenham, the Maidenhead Bridge, Box Tunnel and of course Bristol Temple Meads station.

When the line was constructed, he used his 'broad gauge' measurement rather than the 'standard gauge', pointing out that the larger gauge line would accommodate faster and bigger locomotives, with less risk of them coming off the rails on bends. The line opened in 1844 and it was soon obvious that there was a problem. When it met with the Gloucester to Bristol line, which used the smaller gauge line designed by Stephenson, passengers were obliged to alight from the carriages on one line to join a different train on the other line.

This situation was to become known as the 'Gauge War' and it was eventually resolved by Parliament.

Bristol Temple Meads station

Built for the Great Western Railway between 1839 and 1841, the original Bristol Temple Meads station was designed by Isambard Kingdom Brunel, who at the time was the railway's engineer.

Temple Meads station today is not the same station that Brunel designed and built. Looking at the station now, the original part is on the left before you actually enter the station area.

The old station was built on a huge, cathedral-style scale and yet it was completed in just two years. It would be another 14 years before Paddington station in London was built, the only railway building that could be considered anywhere near such a masterpiece.

Brunel had to take into consideration a number of design issues that had never been tackled in a single building project before. Not only did he have to design an engine shed, passenger hall, ticket office and goods area, but there also had to be stabling for hundreds of horses, along with an engineering shop.

To add to his problems, he was not allowed to build the station within the old medieval city walls, so he chose to position it in the water meadows of Temple Parish, which stood just beyond the Temple Gate of the city. When it was completed, the roof of the passenger shed, which was constructed of timber and iron, had the widest single span of its time.

Why Temple Meads?

The name Temple Meads comes from the nearby Temple Church, while the word 'meads' is a derivation of 'mæd', an Old English variation of 'mædwe' meaning meadow. This refers to the water meadows alongside the River Avon, once part of Temple parish.

Clifton Suspension Bridge

Work on the supporting piers was started in 1831 but was halted when funds ran out. The final design was modified by the Institute of Civil Engineers prior to completion in 1864 as a memorial to Brunel. The bridge is held by chains, anchored 55 feet below the road. The road is 3 feet higher on the Clifton side to create a level appearance.

Dimensions	
Total length	1,351 feet
Total span	702 feet
Width	31 feet
Height of piers	86 feet

The Gauge War

With the popularity of, and huge increase in, passenger travel, more and more railway lines were being laid down. The railway system had little control and railway companies – of which there was no shortage – were keen to extend their lines in all directions and as far as possible; there was huge competition.

There was one problem though: the gauge of the lines that were being laid – rail transport track gauge is the spacing between the rails and is measured between the inner faces of the load-bearing rails. During this early period, there were basically two opposing sizes: that of the Great Western Railway which adopted the 'broad gauge' of 7 feet, and then that of the 'standard gauge' at 4 feet, 8½ inches – obviously this constituted quite a large discrepancy!

Confusion at the end of the gauge at Gloucester station.

When these two gauges met there was quite clearly an impasse as the locomotives could not pass from one to the other. This was more of a distraction for the passengers than anything else as they would have to dismount from their carriage on one line, to board another carriage on the other so that they could continue their journey.

Something quite clearly had to be done to resolve the situation, and so in 1845 a Royal Commission looked into the problem. A questionnaire of 6,500 questions was distributed to railway engineers and, when all the answers were collated, which must have been quite a task, a decision was made. The 'standard gauge', which had originally been adopted by

The GWR's Fire Fly *exits her shed. Although she is a 'broad gauge' loco with the wider rail size, the smaller 'standard gauge' rails are also evident.*

Stephenson, was to become the overall gauge for the railways; the Gauge Act was passed by Parliament in 1846, although the Great Western Railway kept its 'broad gauge' until 1892, after which it too changed to 'standard gauge'.

Fire Fly class

The Star class locomotives were introduced to the Great Western railway by Daniel Gooch and were a great success. His successor would be a class based on North Star, but which would be fitted with larger boilers; enter the Fire Fly class, which was introduced into service between March 1840 and December 1842.

The *Fire Fly* was a 'broad gauge' 2-2-2 configuration steam locomotive which was used for passenger services. Sixty-one similar locomotives were to follow, all of the same designated class.

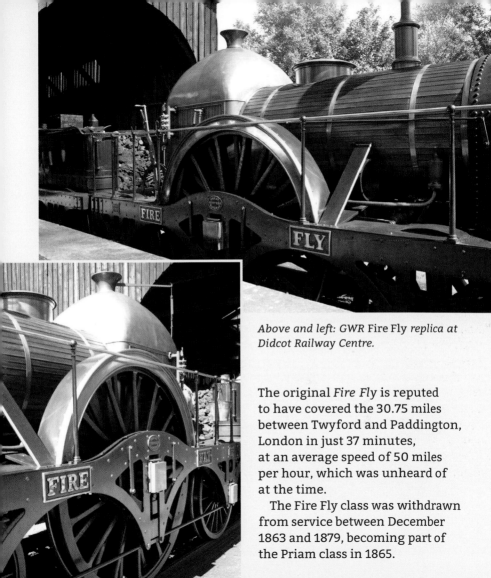

Above and left: GWR Fire Fly *replica at Didcot Railway Centre.*

The original *Fire Fly* is reputed to have covered the 30.75 miles between Twyford and Paddington, London in just 37 minutes, at an average speed of 50 miles per hour, which was unheard of at the time.

The Fire Fly class was withdrawn from service between December 1863 and 1879, becoming part of the Priam class in 1865.

Crampton design

Thomas Russell Crampton, an engineer born in Broadstairs, Kent, in the south of England, was another designer who was working on the large boiler idea. He had spent part of his life designing 'broad gauge' locomotives that were faster and superior to the 'standard gauge' engines in an effort to convince the Board of Trade and Members of Parliament that broad gauge was the way to go.

Patented in 1843, the main feature of the Crampton locomotives

Seen here in the Mulhouse Museum, France, is No. 80 Le Continent, *built for the CF Paris–Strasbourg line in 1852.*

was the position of the driving axle behind the firebox. This allowed the use of large driving wheels, no matter the size or height of the boiler, while at the same time preserving a low centre of gravity.

When Crampton left the Great Western Railway, he publicized his new engine and, before long, was approached by the British managers of the Namur and Liège Railway in Belgium. Although Crampton locomotives were used by some British railways, they were more popular in Europe, in particular Germany, Belgium and France.

Crampton also designed engines for the 'standard gauge' and in 1847

delivered *Liverpool*, which incorporated his ideas. It became the most powerful engine of its time, able to haul 180 tons at 50 miles per hour.

By 1878 all express trains on the Eastern Railway of France were Crampton designs; Crampton-designed engines were also supplied to Prussian Eastern Railways.

The Big Four 1923–47

By the mid-1800s the railways in Britain were having a huge impact on industrialization, with transportation costs having been lowered to the benefit of industries that needed to move their goods around. In turn, the railways benefited and the demand for more goods and supplies was increasing at a good rate.

The railway system had been cleverly integrated and was no longer a patchwork of different lines with different gauges. It was a well-engineered system that proved to be fast, on time and inexpensive for the movement of not only freight, but also people, to most cities and even to rural destinations.

It seemed like the system was growing by the day and by 1880 there were 13,500 locomotives, each carrying an average of 97,800 passengers or 31,500 tons of freight per year.

During this period, the government had started to interest itself more in the railways, in particular when it came to safety matters. The Railway Inspectorate was established in 1840 and in 1844 a bill was put forward suggesting that the state purchase the railways.

During the First World War, when the whole network was brought under government control, Conservative members of the wartime coalition government resisted calls for the formal nationalization. But after the war on 1 January 1923, almost all the railway companies were grouped into what became known as the 'Big Four', which consisted of the Great Western Railway (GWR), the London and North Eastern Railway (LNER), the London, Midland and Scottish Railway (LMS) and Southern Railway (SR).

The London, Midland and Scottish Railway (LMS)

The LMS came into existence on 1 January 1923 under the Railways Act of 1921, which required the grouping of over 120 separate railways into just four – the LMS being the largest of the 'Big Four'.

The companies that merged to create the LMS included: London and North Western Railway; Midland Railway; the Lancashire and Yorkshire Railway (which had previously merged with the London and North Western Railway on 1 January 1922); North Staffordshire Railway; several Scottish railway companies (including the Caledonian Railway); and numerous other smaller ventures such as the Furness Railway.

There were also some 24 subsidiary railways, which were leased or worked by the above-mentioned companies, a large number of joint railways and three railways in Ireland. It became the world's largest transport organization, the largest commercial enterprise in the British Empire as well as being the United Kingdom's second-largest employer after the Post Office.

LMS Stanier class 5 4-6-0 No. 44806 was built at Derby in 1944 and is a preserved locomotive. It is now part of the North Yorkshire Moors Railway.

It was only the arrival of the new chief mechanical engineer, William Stanier, who had been headhunted from the Great Western Railway that brought about unification and stability within the company. Prior to his arrival there had been much infighting between the two main rivals, the Midlands and the North Western.

The LMS was nationalized, along with the other members of the 'Big Four' in 1948.

Stoke-on-Trent station (LMS)

Stoke-on-Trent station buildings, situated in Winton Square, are Victorian and were opened on 9 October 1848. The station was built by the North Staffordshire Railway Company (NSR) and until the amalgamation of 1923, when the NSR was incorporated into the LMS, housed the company's boardroom and its principal offices.

Winton Square is described as Britain's only piece of major town planning undertaken by a railway company specifically to offset a station building. The station is a Grade II-listed building, made of dark red brick with black diapering and stone dressings. It has three Dutch-style gables with a prominent, first-floor bay window, which is decoratively mullioned and a parapet overhead bearing the NSR's coat of arms. Either side of the bay window is a terrace, which runs across the top of an arcade of Tuscan columns flanking seven arches.

48305 LMS Stanier class 8F

The London, Midland and Scottish Railway's 8F class 2-8-0 heavy freight locomotive is a class of steam locomotive designed for hauling heavy freight.

When World War Two broke out, the 8F was chosen to be the country's standard freight train design, with the War Department ordering 208 to be built by Beyer Peacock and the North British Locomotive Company, while also requisitioning a further 51.

The 8F continued to be built until 1943 when the less expensive WD Austerity 2-8-0 took over; production for the domestic market continued after the war until 1946.

Service abroad

The War Department had ordered 8Fs for service in support of the British Expeditionary Force (BEF), but they were not delivered until after the fall of France. However, most of them did see wartime military service overseas in Egypt, Palestine, Iran and Italy.

Accident

On 9 February 1957, locomotive No. 48188 was hauling a freight train that ran away due to the

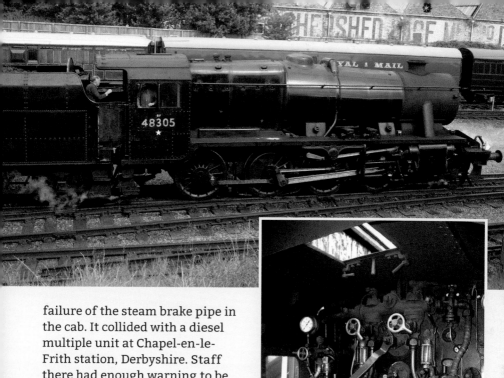

failure of the steam brake pipe in the cab. It collided with a diesel multiple unit at Chapel-en-le-Frith station, Derbyshire. Staff there had enough warning to be able to evacuate the train before the collision. Driver John Axon had remained with the freight and was killed. He was awarded a posthumous George Cross.

BRUSH WITH FAME

8F No. 48600 was used in the 1953 Glenn Ford film *Time Bomb*, also called *Terror on a Train*.

Leander – Jubilee class locomotive

Leander is a Jubilee class locomotive with the number 5690; she was built at Crewe in March 1936. The name derives from HMS *Leander*, which in turn was named after the Greek hero Leander, who was involved in a tragic love story.

The LMS Jubilee class locomotives were designed for mainline passenger services and 191 examples were manufactured between 1934 and 1936.

Following nationalization in 1948, *Leander* was renumbered 45690 by British Railways and based out of the former engine shed at Bristol, Barrow Road.

Leander was withdrawn in 1964 and sold to Woodham Brothers' scrapyard in Wales, only to be saved in May 1972 and restored by the Leander Locomotive Society at Derby.

Austerity class

Based on the LMS class 8F, the Austerity 2-8-0 was ordered for war work by the War Department. This heavy freight steam loco was introduced in 1943 and a total of 935 were built, which also makes this one of the most popular classes of British steam locomotive.

Originally designed by R. A. Riddles, these engines were modified at a time when low cost rather than durability was the priority. For example, a simpler boiler construction featuring steel rather than the more expensive copper was used.

Locomotives had their War Department numbers increased by 70,000 before being shipped to mainland Europe, although those made after September 1944 already had their new designation. All but three saw service with the British Army in mainland Europe after D-Day.

After the war, some engines were re-classified and, in 1946, 12 were exported to Hong Kong for the Kowloon–Canton Railway. Another 184 locomotives remained in the Netherlands for Nederlandse Spoorwegen, while one went to the United States Army Transportation Corps in exchange for a USATC S160 class locomotive in the post-war exchange of WD and USATC locomotives.

Locomotive No. 90733 is a War Department 'Austerity' 2-8-0 class heavy freight engine introduced in 1943.

LMS 47324 Jinty

Often referred to as a Jinty, the LMS Fowler 3F 0-6-0T locomotive is seen as the ultimate development of the Midland Railways' six-coupled tank engines. Between 1924 and 1931, 422 Jinty locomotives were built, the first being originally numbered 13000, before the entire fleet was renumbered into the 7200 series in 1932.

During World War Two, these engines were chosen by the War Department as their standard shunting locomotive. Some were even dispatched to France prior to its fall in 1940.

At the start of nationalization in 1948, the remaining 417 engines passed into the hands of British Railways and were renumbered between 47260 and 47681. Many lasted until the end of steam, but half had been withdrawn by 1964.

No. 47324 was built by the North British Locomotive Company at their Hyde Park Works in June 1926 and took the LMS number 16407. She was withdrawn in December 1966 and made her last journey to Woodham Brothers' scrapyard in Wales.

Due to their large numbers, late withdrawals and renowned performances, nine of these engines (plus a spare set of frames and a boiler from 47564) have been preserved.

L&YR class 25 lococomotive No. 957

New locomotive superintendent William Barton Wright introduced the Lancashire & Yorkshire Railway class 25 0-6-0 locomotives in 1876; 280 examples were eventually built. Out of this number, 230 were converted to saddle tanks by John Aspinall, which then became L&YR class 23.

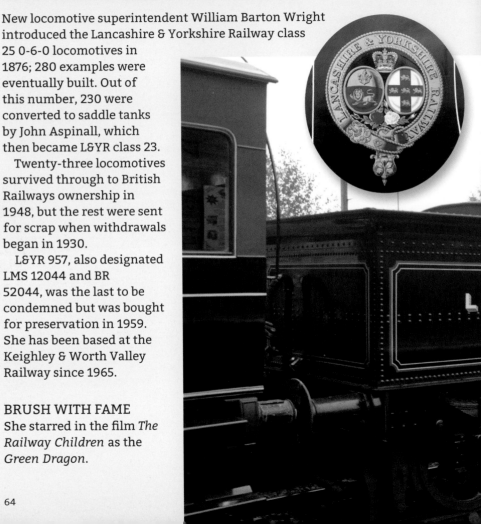

Twenty-three locomotives survived through to British Railways ownership in 1948, but the rest were sent for scrap when withdrawals began in 1930.

L&YR 957, also designated LMS 12044 and BR 52044, was the last to be condemned but was bought for preservation in 1959. She has been based at the Keighley & Worth Valley Railway since 1965.

BRUSH WITH FAME
She starred in the film *The Railway Children* as the *Green Dragon*.

Stanier Class Five

Often referred to as the Black Five, the William Stanier design was introduced to the LMS in 1934; a total of 832 were built. Many survived until the end of steam in 1968 and to date eight have been preserved, of which 45110 is one.

A very versatile mixed-traffic locomotive, the first 20 were ordered from the Crewe Works, while a further 80 were constructed at the Vulcan Foundry, which is where the original, number 5020, was also made in 1934. 5110, as it was numbered during the LMS days, was built at the Vulcan Foundry in 1935.

This locomotive was one of three of the class that hauled the 'Fifteen Guinea Special', British Railways' last steam-hauled passenger train on 11 August 1968. It was then purchased for preservation by the Severn Valley Railway and is generally based at their Bewdley depot.

Fowler 7F 2-8-0 No. 88

A class of locomotive for heavy freight work, the 7F 2-8-0 of the Somerset and Dorset Joint Railway (S&DJR) was designed by James Clayton, a draughtsman at Derby. Eleven were constructed in two batches during 1914 and 1925.

The first batch of locomotives had right-hand-driving positions, but the second batch had the driver on the left. No. 88 (later 53808) was built by Robert Stephenson & Company, making up part of the second batch in 1925.

No. 88 was withdrawn in 1964, along with the remaining three. Two have survived, 88 on the West Somerset Railway and 89 at the Midland Railway, Butterley.

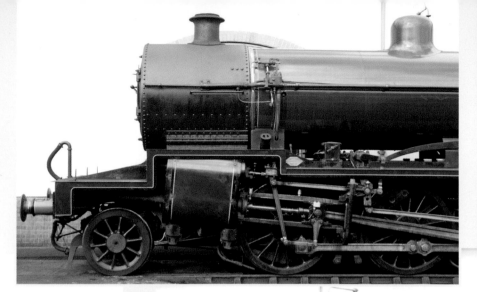

Ivatt class 2 2-6-2T

Introduced between 1946 and 1952, the Ivatt Class 2 2-6-2T was a light 'mixed-traffic' locomotive based on the LMS Stanier 2-6-2T, which in turn was based on the LMS Fowler 2-6-2T. Ten examples were built by the LMS prior to nationalization and numbered 1200–1209, after which British Railways added a further 120 which meant they were numbered 41210–41329 (BR having added a '4' at the front of each number). All except the last ten, which were built at Derby, were made at Crewe, with number 41272 being the 700th locomotive to be manufactured on the premises.

When initially preserved, No. 41241 was painted in a generic maroon livery with K&WVR on the tanks; it was later restored to more conventional BR black. She is particularly associated with the Keighley & Worth Valley Railway.

Creation of the London & North Eastern Railway

The LNER was the second-largest of the 'Big Four' created by the Railways Act of 1921. It was formed through the amalgamation of a variety of constituent railways: Great Eastern Railway; Great Central Railway; Great Northern Railway; Great North of Scotland Railway; Hull & Barnsley Railway; North British Railway and North Eastern Railway.

Its network embraced a total route mileage of 6,590 and the organization owned 7,700 locomotives, 20,000 coaching vehicles, 29,700 freight vehicles, 140 pieces of electric rolling stock, 6 electric locomotives, 10 rail motorcars, 6 turbine and 36 other steamers. Also part of the package were a number of river boats and steamers, docks and harbours in various locations, some Eastern Scottish ports, Harwich and London wharves and piers in several places along with 23 hotels. In 1936 the largest UK joint railway, the Great Northern Joint Railway, also became part of the LNER.

Despite being the second-largest of the 'Big Four', it was the poorest, but it was still famous for its prestigious high-speed trains. Much of its income came from the coalfields of North East England.

As with the other 'Big Four' companies, it was nationalized in 1948.

LNER ex-NER Z10 class 4-4-2 Atlantic with a plane passing low overhead, c. 1923.

Thompson class B1

Designed by Edward Thompson, class B1 No. 1264 – later changed to 61264 by British Railways – was built as part of a batch of 1264 in 1947 by the North British Locomotive Company.

She was allocated Parkseston Quay shed near Harwich where she remained for 13 years, passing into the ownership of British Railways in 1948. In November 1960 she was transferred to Colwick Depot near Nottingham and remained there until she was withdrawn in December 1965. It was not quite the end of her working days; a transfer to departmental stock saw her renumbered 29 in the Eastern Region departmental stock series. Here, she was used as a mobile boiler for heating carriages.

She was withdrawn from departmental stock in July 1967 and a year later was sold for scrap to Woodham Brothers in Wales. Luckily, she was saved from scrapping in 1973 and became the 83rd engine to leave Woodham Brothers and go into preservation.

No. 61264 is one of two surviving Thompson class B1s, but the only LNER-built example, the other being BR-built 61306 *Mayflower*.

Raven 63395 Q6 class

Designed by Vincent Raven, the T2 0-8-0 or Q6 locomotives, as they later became known, were built to handle the heavy goods trains of the North Eastern Railway. In total, 120 were built at the NER's Darlington Works between 1913 and 1918; they proved to be very capable engines right through to the end of steam in the North in 1967. As class T2 No. 2238, locomotive 63395 was completed by the NER at Darlington North Road Works on 3 November 1918, one of eight built that year.

On 14 June 1959, 63395 was transferred once more to Darlington Bank Top, and then to Consett, before the engine was finally sent to Sunderland South Dock on 23 May 1965. From here, the Q6 worked south to Vane Tempest, Seaham, Teesside and South Hetton, and northwards to the Tyne, fittingly ending her days where they had begun almost 50 years before.

During the final days of steam operation in County Durham and Northumberland, one of the last survivors was 63395, and following withdrawal she was moved to Tyne Dock to await preservation.

Loco No. 63395 is currently preserved as LNER No. 2238 on the North Yorkshire Moors Railway.

The Great Marquess

The class K4 2-6-0 steam locomotives of the LNER were designed by Sir Nigel Gresley for the steep gradients and sharp curves of the West Highland line to Mallaig via Fort William.

The passenger service on this route prior to 1924 was pulled by D33, *Glen*, a 4-4-0 configuration locomotive, occasionally assisted by double-headers. In 1924, the Great Northern Railway sent 14 K2s to the rescue, which solved the problem for a while.

After much experimenting with steam pressure and tractive adhesion, the prototype K4, numbered 3441 and named *Loch Long*, went into service on 28 January 1937. She was soon showing her true potential by pulling 300-ton trains with a maximum speed of 60 miles per hour on the level. Five more engines were built between 1938 and 1939, all named after Highland chieftains and grandees.

Sir Nigel Gresley

Probably the most famous designer for the LNER was Sir Nigel Gresley, who became chief mechanical engineer of the Great Northern Railway (GNR) in 1911, which was subsequently incorporated into the LNER.

Gresley was born in 1876 and raised in Derbyshire. He went to school at Marlborough College, following which he became an apprentice at Crewe Works. He moved to the Lancashire and York Railway in 1898 and resigned from there in 1905 to become the superintendent of the Great Northern Railway carriage and wagon department.

His early locomotives included a large-boiler, three-cylinder, 2-6-0 K3, which was introduced in 1920. Due to the intervention of World War One, Gresley's express passenger designs had to be halted; he returned to them in

1920, when he also introduced his conjugated valve-gear system. April 1922 saw the first Gresley Pacific class A1, 1470 Great Northern, enter service.

Displayed at the 1924 and 1925 British Empire exhibitions and probably the best-known locomotive in the world was the 4472 *Flying Scotsman*. This was the locomotive that, while pulling a dynamometer car, became the first steam locomotive to record an authenticated 100 miles per hour.

Sir Nigel became one of Britain's most famous locomotive designers and his line of 'Pacifics', which started life with the GNR A1, later upgraded to A3, reached their prime with the well-respected and beautiful A4s.

It was one of these A4s that broke the world speed record for a steam engine in 1938, a record which incidentally still stands today! *Mallard* was the locomotive and it reached 125 miles per hour, although there is still some talk of 126 miles per hour, which even Sir Nigel Gresley refused to acknowledge.

Gresley went on to introduce the V2, one of his most successful engines along with the Mikado engines.

The Sir Nigel Gresley A4 locomotive

The A4s are probably the most famous of all the LNER Express Pacific designs and it is easy to understand why. Their distinctive streamline design was all new at the time and they symbolized 1930s elegance and luxury at high speed.

The 60007 carries a plaque that confirms it as the holder of the post-war steam record of 112 miles per hour, obtained on 23 May 1959. The

Sir Nigel Gresley was the 100th Pacific built and, as per the earlier Pacifics, it only had one chimney, having been fitted with a double chimney and Kylchap double blastpipe on 13 December 1957.

The end of the line came for number 60007, the *Sir Nigel Gresley*, in 2015. The A4 class steam engine is going temporarily, one hopes, into retirement. Its last outing was as the 'Cathedral Express to Edinburgh', which ran from Kings Cross in London. It will be missed.

Left: The Sir Nigel Gresley *leaves Grosmont on the North Yorkshire Moors Railway.*

Opposite top: No. 60007 makes a refuelling stop as admiring crowds look on. Note how the streamlining panel is raised, revealing the original front end.

Below: The Sir Nigel Gresley *is ready to depart.*

LNER class A4 4464 Bittern

Bittern was built for the LNER in 1937 at Doncaster Works as works number 1866. Then things become a little confusing; she was originally numbered 4464, then this was changed to 19 under the LNER 1946 renumbering scheme. After nationalization in 1948, British Rail added 60000 to her number, so she became 60019 on 10 October 1948.

One of six to survive for preservation, *Bittern* is a Pacific 4-6-2 locomotive to the same design by Sir Nigel Gresley as the more famous A4 *Mallard*. While in preservation, she has also worn several of her scrapped classmates' numbers, including the first of the A4 class 2509 Silver Link.

Like most other A4s, *Bittern* was fitted with side valances and a single chimney from new. She has outlived 14 boilers in her career, but has had only one tender of the non-corridor type, although during preservation that was changed to a corridor version.

Initially based at Heaton in Newcastle, *Bittern* served the *Flying Scotsman* train down to Kings Cross. She suffered collision damage which led to a general overhaul in 1938. During World War Two, she was used beyond her limits, pulling longer-than-normal, heavy passenger trains and also heavy freight and coal trains. All this and the lack of maintenance took its toll and after the war she was found to be in a poor state.

With better maintenance under British Railways, these fast A4 class locomotives returned to their pre-war high-speed express lines. Sadly, the steam-based services were soon replaced by diesel locomotives and *Bittern* was exiled to Scotland and put in storage. The final day in service for *Bittern* was 3 September 1966.

Union of South Africa

No. 60009 *Union of South Africa* was built for the LNER in 1937 and originally took the number 4488. Although originally allocated the moniker *Osprey* in 1937, the name was changed to celebrate the newly formed Union of South Africa. With the troubles that occurred during the early 1990s, the *Osprey* nameplates were refitted to the locomotive for political reasons, although it has since reverted once again to *Union of South Africa*.

Starting her working life at the Haymarket shed in Edinburgh, she made her only transfer to Aberdeen on 20 May 1962. On 24 October 1964, she hauled the last steam-hauled train from Kings Cross and on 1 June 1966 60009 was withdrawn from British Railways service.

LNER Thompson/Peppercorn class K1

Arthur Peppercorn was principal assistant to Edward Thompson at the London and North Eastern Railway (LNER) and took over as chief mechanical engineer. Although the design of the K1 is attributed to Peppercorn, its history goes back to the Great Northern Railway (GNR) and Sir Nigel Gresley. His first design, which was much influenced by the North American 2-6-0 wheel configuration, was introduced as the GNR class H2, later becoming the LNER class K1, with final development into the K4.

Thompson took over from Gresley after his death in 1941 and continued to make modifications on the K4 prototype *MacCain Mor*. These were successful modifications and were further enhanced when Peppercorn took over from Thompson.

Seventy of these 2-6-0 mixed-traffic locomotives were placed with the North British Locomotive Company of Glasgow and became the last steam locomotives to be built to LNER design, although delivered under British Railways patronage. They entered service between May 1949 and March 1950.

The Peppercorn K1s worked mostly over ex-LNER territory, but were chiefly associated with North East England and the West Highland Line. They had a very short working life and were withdrawn between 1962 and 1967, with just the last one being saved from destruction. No. 62005, *Lord of the Isles*, has been preserved and is based at the North Yorkshire Moors Railway, but spends most of its time on the summer Fort William–Mallaig Jacobite service.

4771 Green Arrow

LNER class V2 2-6-2 steam locomotive number 4771 *Green Arrow* was built in June 1936 for the London and North Eastern Railway (LNER) at Doncaster Works. One of Sir Nigel Gresley's most successful designs, the V2 became the LNER's best-known mixed-traffic locomotive type.

Named after an express freight service, *Green Arrow* was the first one to be built and is the only surviving member of its class. It was initially allotted the number 637 and fitted with curved nameplates over the middle driving wheels. Before it went into service it received the number 4771, but it went through a variety of number changes before finally receiving the number 60800 from British Railways in February 1949.

No. 4771 was withdrawn in 1962 and selected for preservation. It was sent for restoration to the Doncaster Works, the work being completed in April 1963.

BRUSH WITH FAME

Green Arrow appears in The Railway Series book *Thomas and the Great Railway Show*, double-heading a steam special to Scarborough with Thomas the Tank Engine.

Morayshire class D49

From the late 1800s, the majority of Scottish express trains were hauled by tender locomotives with a four-wheeled bogie leading four driving wheels. By 1923, when the railways were reorganized and grouped into the 'Big Four', these engines were starting to show their age.

Nigel Gresley, who was then locomotive superintendent for the LNER, started to investigate the possibility of a new locomotive that would be suitable for express passenger service for intermediate duties in the North Eastern and Scottish areas.

His design was presented to the Locomotive Works at Darlington, and in October 1927 the first of his new class of 4-4-0 locomotives was submitted. A total of 76 engines were manufactured until 1935, with

Morayshire being outshopped in February of 1928.

No. 246 *Morayshire* was based at various locations – Dundee, Perth, Haymarket and St Margaret's – and was withdrawn as the last of its class in July 1961. Several more moves were made after this and restoration work carried out before she was presented to the Royal Scottish Museum in Edinburgh. *Morayshire* is now operational on the Bo'ness & Kinneil Railway.

4472 Flying Scotsman

The *Flying Scotsman* is probably the most famous steam locomotive in the world and its number 4472 is recognized by enthusiasts everywhere. Built orignally as an A1 locomotive, it hasn't always carried that number; when built, it was given the GNR number 1472. Both the name and the number were changed when it became the LNER flagship locomotive at the British Empire Exhibition at Wembley in 1924 and 1925.

This class A3 4-6-2 Pacific was built in 1923 at Doncaster Works to a design by Sir Nigel Gresley and extensively used for long-distance express trains for the LNER and its successors, British Railways Eastern and North-Eastern regions, in particular the London to Edinburgh Flying Scotsman service, from which it got its name.

The *Flying Scotsman* retired from regular service in 1963 and while it hauled enthusiast specials in the UK, it has also travelled extensively to America, Canada and Australia. During its working life, it covered a staggering 2,076,000 miles.

BRUSH WITH FAME

One of its first film appearances was in the 1929 film *The Flying Scotsman*, which featured an entire sequence set aboard the locomotive. In 1986, the *Flying Scotsman* appeared in a British Rail TV advert. This was far from its only public appearance: it's been seen on coins and in computer games, and in many other places. It's no wonder the locomotive is so well loved.

Creation of Southern Rail (SR)

As with the other members of the 'Big Four', Southern Railway was an amalgamation of several local railways of which the main constituents were: London and South Western Railway; London, Brighton and South Coast Railway; constituents of the South Eastern and Chatham Railway; three Isle of Wight Railways; and Lynton & Barnstaple Railway.

They owned tracks adding up to 2,186 route miles (virtually monopolizing the south of the country); 2,390 locomotives; 10,800 coaching vehicles; 37,500 freight vehicles; 460 electric vehicles; 14 rail motorcars; 38 large turbines and other steamers; assorted other vessels and 3.5 miles of canals.

They also owned docks, harbours and equipment in several south coast towns, ten large hotels and London termini, including the largest London railway station, Waterloo. In addition, there were Victoria, Charing Cross, Cannon Street, and the oldest London railway station, London Bridge. Considering this long list, it might seem rather unlikely, but Southern Railway was the smallest of the 'Big Four'.

This amazing 1930s scene shows photographer Arthur Mace at his best. The location is Folkestone harbour and the engine is one of Stirling's class R Domeless 0-6-0Ts.

Southern Railway 4-6-2 West Country class

Blackmoor Vale was designed by Oliver Vaughan Snell Bulleid, the chief mechanical engineer of the Southern Railway, and was built to order at their works in Brighton in 1946. Generally known as the Light Pacifics, the class numbered 110 locomotives which were made distinctive by their air-smoothed casing over the boiler.

Members of the class were named after West Country locations, and also after RAF air squadrons, fighters and personalities involved with the RAF and its war effort, the Battle of Britain class.

Blackmoor Vale was initially numbered 21C123 in the Bulleid numbering system, but after the formation of British Railways in 1948 she was renumbered in the Southern Railway's classification system as No. 34023, with the distinctive Southern roundel still on the smokebox and the lettering 'British Railways' on the tender sides.

No. 34023 was withdrawn in July 1967 and purchased by the Bulleid Preservation Society.

Top: Blackmoor Vale *steams across beautiful Sussex countryside. Far left: Many West Country locomotives carried the coat of arms of the town or region they were associated with. Left: The cab of* Blackmoor Vale. *Above: A truly radical design in her day,* Blackmoor Vale *awaits her turn at Sheffield Park station on the Bluebell Railway.*

Wadebridge locomotive No. 34007

Wadebridge was completed at Brighton in August 1945 and is a West Country class engine designed by O. V. S. Bulleid. The West Country class engines were designed to be a lighter version of the 'Merchant Navy' locomotives, also built by Bulleid. These new locomotives were built to be more versatile and able to run on the lesser-used lines of Southern Railways.

Often referred to as 'Spam Cans', due to their shape, these locomotives were very different from anything around at the time. Wadebridge is fairly unique in that it was not rebuilt and retains its original air-smoothing cases and chain-driven valve gear.

Originally numbered 21C107, *Wadebridge* started its life at Exmoor Junction, after which she moved to Nine Elms in 1951, where she received her new number 34007. The original designation 21C107 includes references to the axles in the leading bogie ('2'); '1' refers to the trailing wheels and 'C' to the three pairs of coupled wheels. The West Country class started at 101.

Salisbury was her last home before being withdrawn in October 1965. She was moved to Barry scrapyard in Wales in 1966, having covered a staggering 823,193 miles while in service. She was rescued from destruction in 1981 and is now happily serving the Mid-Hants Railway on the Watercress Line.

35005 Merchant Navy class

Initially known as the 21C1 class, but formally known as the Bulleid Pacifics, the Southern Railways Merchant Navy class, like its sister locomotives the West Country class, were air-smoothed 4-6-2 steam locomotives.

The first members of the class were constructed during the Second World War, and the last of the 30 locomotives in 1949. They were named after the Merchant Navy shipping lines involved in the Battle of the Atlantic and then later those which used Southampton docks, which Southern Railways owned at the time.

30926 Repton – Schools class

The last locomotive in Britain to be designed with the 4-4-0 wheel alignment, the V class, or more commonly known Schools class locomotives, were designed by Richard Maunsell for Southern Railways. All the class, of which there were 40, were named after English public schools, hence the class name; they were also the most powerful class of 4-4-0 ever produced in Europe.

Ex-Southern/British Rail 926/30926, *Repton* entered service on the Bournemouth route in May 1934. One of the last of the class to be overhauled by British Railways in 1960, she was considered a good choice for preservation. In December 1962 the engine was withdrawn from service and, after being overhauled at Eastleigh in 1966, she relocated to the USA, where she was donated by the purchaser to Steamtown USA in Vermont. Steamtown loaned the engine to the Cape Breton Steam Railway in Canada and in 1989 she was sold again, returning to the UK and the North Yorkshire Moors Railway.

The Bluebell Terrier Stepney

The first batch of A1 class 0-6-0T steam locomotives, generally known
as Terriers and designed by William Stroudley, were started in 1872 and
continued to be built until 1880. It is quite incredible to think that some are
still running after nearly 150 years.

They were intended for lightweight 'block trains' (a train in which all
cars or wagons carry the same commodity and are shipped from the same
origin to the same destination, without being split up or stored en route),

in particular in the London area where the A1 Terrier could handle the light construction of the rails and their poor foundation.

By the end of the 19th century, the requirement for so many Terriers had declined and many of these little engines were by now starting to show their age; many were scrapped and others sold off. Some survived on branch lines, but numbers started to dwindle and eventually *Stepney*, too, was withdrawn. Fortunately, she was saved from demolition and allocated the Hayling Island Branch, before ending up at the Bluebell Railway, Sussex.

Fenchurch

The London, Brighton & South Coast Railway A1 Stroudley Terrier 0-6-0T 672 named *Fenchurch* was built in 1872 and after some 25 years working was sold to the Newhaven Harbour Company in 1898.

The Bluebell Railway bought *Fenchurch* in 1964 as a working engine – at 92 years old, she was the oldest engine to have been used on British Railways. She kept going until 1970, when she was overhauled for her centenary celebrations in 1972.

Maunsell U class 1638

Designed by Richard Maunsell, the Southern Railway U class 2-6-0 Mogul steam locomotives were destined for passenger duties on the Southern Railway, cross-country and semi-fast express routes.

Locomotive No. 1638 was outshopped from Ashford on 9 May 1931 and was initially sent to Redhill. Following the electrification of the Brighton line in 1933, she was reallocated to Guildford.

When withdrawn in 1964, she had had ten major overhauls and covered aproximately 915,000 miles in her 33 years of service.

The 114th engine to leave the Woodham Brothers' scrapyard in Barry, Wales, U class No. 1638 moved on to the Bluebell Railway, arriving on 30 June 1980. For the next 13 years, she sat in Turners sidings at Sheffield Park. Restoration was then carried out and she started her service with the Bluebell in February 2006.

Wainwright 01 class

Number 65 was built at Ashford Works in September 1896, initially as a 0 class locomotive. In 1908 she went through a rebuild and was redesignated 01 class. These locomotives had a very low axle weight and due to their initial design were far better equipped to travel on the lines than heavier and larger locomotives.

Following World War One, 65 was based at Ashford and could be seen regularly at Folkestone harbour. After nationalization, she

received the number 31065, and kept working in the Ashford area up to the 1950s. She also had her moment of glory when she double-headed with C class 592 and worked the final service on the Hawkhurst branch. Thirteen days later, she herself was withdrawn from service after a very reasonable 66 years and 1,388,000 miles of service. Fortunately, she was bought and saved in 1963 and is now a stalwart on the Bluebell Railway.

Creation of the Great Western Railway (GWR)

The Great Western Railway (GWR) linked London with the Midlands, the south-west and west of England; it also covered most of Wales. Engineered by Isambard Kingdom Brunel, it was founded in 1833, received its Act of Parliament in 1835 and ran its first train just three years later in 1838.

Unlike most of the other lines, Brunel chose a 'broad gauge' for his lines, which later had to be changed after an Act of Parliament decided that the 'standard' gauge would be used nationally. The last 'broad gauge' train operated in 1892.

The GWR gained many different nicknames – 'God's Wonderful Railway' and the 'Great Way Round' were just two – but most of all it was known as the 'Holiday Line'. The reason for this was that it transported people to and from many Bristol Channel resorts in the West Country and also along the far south-west coast of England.

Many of its steam locomotives were built at their workshops in Swindon and were generally very easy to spot. They were painted a very familiar Brunswick green and had Great Western, GW or GWR written on the side of the tender in yellow.

When it was amalgamated into the 'Big Four', GWR took in the following: Barry Railway, Wales; Cambrian Railways; Cardiff Railway; Rhymney Railway; Taff Vale Railway; Alexandra (Newport & South Wales) Docks and Railway; and the narrow gauge Corris Railway was also absorbed in 1930.

There was a total route length of 3,800 miles and they also acquired locomotives, tenders, coaching vehicles, freight vehicles, electric vehicles and rail motor cars. There were also canals, turbine and twin-screw steamers, along with many smaller vessels, docks, harbours and equipment at Barry, Cardiff, Fishguard, Newport, Penarth, Plymouth and Port Talbot, not forgetting ten hotels.

Left: GWR Castle class 4-6-0 No. 5025 Chirk Castle *at Birmingham Snow Hill, 1930s.*

Collett 5643

In the railway grouping that happened in 1923, the Great Western Railway (GWR) inherited a large number of run-down locomotives from the various independent South Wales companies, and so there was a real need for new machinery.

 The then chief mechanical engineer, Charles Collett, decided to base these new engines on the very successful 0-6-2T wheel arrangement. Building started at the Swindon Works and the first of 200 locomotives, number 5600, came off the production line in 1924. In October of 1925 5643 came out of the Swindon Works and spent most of her working life in and around South Wales. This class of locomotives featured powerful engines for their size and they became very popular with their crews.

4936 Kinlet Hall

Built in June of 1929 at Swindon Works, Kinlet Hall, number 4936 is a 4-6-0
Hall class locomotive of the Great Western Railway.
She was designed by Charles Collett and
her first allocated destination was Chester.

During her working life, she visited a variety of places: Cardiff Canton, Old Oak Common, Oswestry, Oxley, Oxford, Shrewsbury, Stafford Park Road, Swindon, Truro and, finally, Cardiff East Dock. At the start of World War Two, after a bombing raid on Plymouth in 1941, Kinlet Hall fell into a bomb crater and was severely damaged.

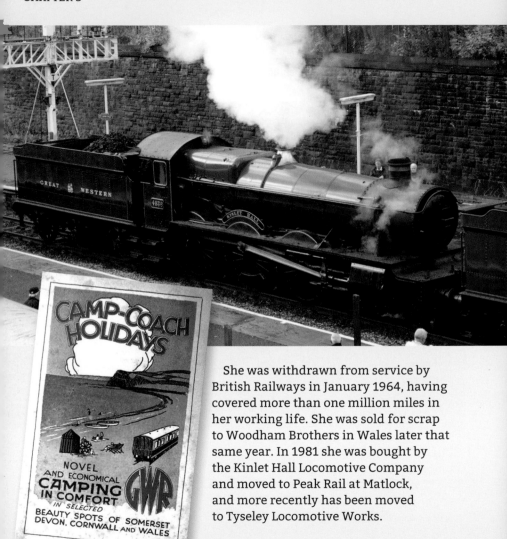

She was withdrawn from service by British Railways in January 1964, having covered more than one million miles in her working life. She was sold for scrap to Woodham Brothers in Wales later that same year. In 1981 she was bought by the Kinlet Hall Locomotive Company and moved to Peak Rail at Matlock, and more recently has been moved to Tyseley Locomotive Works.

Rood Ashton Hall or Albert Hall?

No. 4965 *Rood Ashton Hall* is a 4-6-0 Hall class, Great Western Railway steam locomotive and performs regularly on the Shakespeare Express line between Birmingham and Stratford-upon-Avon.

This locomotive has quite a confusing history as she was previously identified as 4983 *Albert Hall*, having been rebuilt in 1962 using parts from both original engines, *Albert Hall* and *Rood Ashton Hall*; both engines having had their numbers stamped on to their respective parts.

When bought, the owners thought they were buying 4983 *Albert Hall*. Alas, following subsequent restoration, they found that some of the parts had been stamped 4965 and some 4983. *Rood Ashton Hall* now has plates and numbers on one side that say 4983 *Albert Hall* for enthusiasts to see once again, but still hauls *Rood Ashton Hall*'s original tender.

George Jackson Churchward GWR 3440 City of Truro

Part of the Churchward 3700 City class, *City of Truro* number 3440 is a Great Western 4-4-0 configuration locomotive, which was built at the GWR Swindon Works in 1903.

It is suggested that she was the first British locomotive to travel over 100 miles per hour, and was one of the first to do so in the world, but her maximum speed has been the subject of much debate.

Before his death in 1908, Rous-Marten (who wrote for *The Railway Magazine* and other journals and who recorded the time from the train) did in fact name the record-breaking locomotive as *City of Truro*. Official confirmation from the Great Western Railway came in 1922 when they published a letter written in June 1905 by Rous-Marten to James Inglis, the general manager, giving further details:

...*What happened was this: when we topped the Whiteball Summit, we were still doing 63 miles an hour; when we emerged from the Whiteball Tunnel we had reached 80; thenceforward our velocity rapidly and steadily increased, the quarter-mile times diminishing from 11 sec. at the tunnel*

entrance to 10.6 sec., 10.2 sec., 10 sec., 9.8 sec., 9.4 sec., 9.2 sec., and finally to 8.8 sec., this last being equivalent to a rate of 102.3 miles an hour. The two quickest quarters thus occupied exactly 18 sec. for the half-mile, equal to 100 miles an hour. At this time the travelling was so curiously smooth that, but for the sound, it was difficult to believe we were moving at all...

Following the 1904 speed record, 3440 continued in everyday service until she became obsolete in 1931 and was withdrawn from service in March of that year. Because of the engine's importance, GWR's chief mechanical engineer of the time, Charles Collett, asked that she be preserved at the London

& North Eastern Railway's Railway Museum at York. She was donated to the LNER and subsequently displayed at the new museum in York. Because of the dangers of bombing at York during World War Two, the locomotive was evacuated to the small engine shed at Sprouston station (near Kelso) in the Scottish Borders.

Although *City of Truro* was returned to service in 1957 by British Railways Western Region and based at Didcot, she was withdrawn for a second time in 1961. Restoration followed later for her appearance at the GWR's 150th anniversary. As part of the celebrations to mark the founding of the GWR, she was repainted and took on the guise of 3717 once again in 2010. This was the first time she had carried an authentic livery matching her previous status while operating in preservation.

5542 Small Prairie

No. 5542 is a GWR 4575 class 2-6-2T 'Small Prairie' tank engine. She was built in 1928 and withdrawn by British Railways in December 1961, after which she spent the next 14 years in a scrapyard before being acquired for preservation.

Superseding the 4400 class locomotives in 1906, the 4500 class engines took all the best features of their predecessor and added further improvements, such as larger driving wheels. The Great Western branch lines could be steep at times and also quite twisty, but as often described, these engines were the ideal branch-line locomotive.

In fact they became so popular that they could be seen on many of the GWR lines, carrying out all sorts of duties, including freight or service runs on several well-known trains, including pulling the Cambrian Coast Express and shuttling the Cheltenham Flyer. This was one very versatile locomotive.

Locomotive 4141, GWR 5101 class Large Prairie

This locomotive was built in 1946 and is a medium-sized tank engine with a 2-6-2T wheel arrangement, designed for suburban and local passenger trains.

After leaving Swindon in August 1946, 4141 was based at the Gloucester (Horton Road) depot for her entire working life, which lasted just 17 years. In February 1963 she was sent to Barry scrapyard in Wales, but was saved when a Severn Valley Railway (SVR) member expressed an interest in purchasing the locomotive in 1970. With help from the 'Hampton Loade Loco Fund', 4141 arrived on the SVR on 6 January 1973.

No. 4141 moved to Hampton Loade after several months at Bewdley. Restoration was started on an isolated section of track, but progress was slow and by 1988 it had practically stopped. The engine moved away from the SVR before restoration was completed, and she was resold eventually to steam along on the Llangollen Railway in 1998.

In October 2012 the locomotive moved to her latest home, the Epping Ongar Railway, where she arrived in time to be the 'Santa Special'.

Pannier tank engine 0-6-OPT 3738 designed by Charles Collett and built at Swindon.

Great Western Railway 5700 class

The GWR 5700 class – or 57xx class 0-6-0 pannier tank steam locomotives – was manufactured between 1929 and 1950, during which time 863 were built. This makes them the most prolific class of the GWR, and one of the most numerous classes of British steam locomotive.

They worked across most of the GWR network and, following nationalization in 1948, they could also be seen across the British Railways Western Region and several other regions.

Initially designated by GWR as light goods and shunting engines, they were also used for carrying passengers on branch, suburban, and shorter mainline journeys.

As a result of the 1955 Modernization Plan, the 5700 class was withdrawn from BR service between 1956 and 1966. Nineteen withdrawn locomotives were sold to London Transport and industry, of which ten were later preserved, along with six that were retrieved from scrapyards.

GWR 2-8-0 No 3850

The first locomotive to use the 2-8-0 wheel configuration was a prototype of the 28xx class (later designation '2800'), number 97. These were designed by George Jackson Churchward – chief mechanical engineer of the GWR – and, by 1919, a total of 84 had been built at Swindon.

Some 20 years later, a second batch of 83 locomotives was ordered and built between 1938 and 1942. Known as the 2884 class, these were slightly modified versions that Charles Collett, Churchward's successor, had designed.

Constructed as part of the last batch of 23, 3850 was built at Swindon and was turned out on 16 June 1942, painted in wartime black livery. She was sent to her first shed at St Phillip's Marsh, Bristol, after which she was allocated various destinations, working mostly on coal and iron ore duties.

Purchased by Woodham Brothers for scrap, she was sidelined for some 20 years until she was resold on 26 February 1984. She moved to Bishop Lydeard on 3 March that same year, and some months later restoration began at Minehead.

Foxcote Manor

Loco 7822 *Foxcote Manor* is a Manor class locomotive. She was built by British Railways at their Swindon Works in 1950. Had World War Two not intervened, there is a good chance she would have been built several years before, just after the first batch of 20 engines numbered 7800–7819, which were built prior to the war in 1938 and 1939.

With their 4-6-0 configuration and relatively light axle load, the Manor class locomotives of the GWR were versatile and light, but also powerful enough for hauling trains.

No. 7822 began life at Oswestry and hauled passengers and freight through vicinities such as Ellesmere, Shrewsbury, Aberystwyth and Barmouth. She finished her days at Shrewsbury before a final spell at Chester. *Foxcote Manor* was consigned to the scrapyard in Barry, Wales in 1965 and would have been cut up if she had been nearer the front of the queue – thankfully, 7822 was restored by the Foxcote Manor Society, initially at Oswestry, and later at Llangollen.

GWR 3802 Heavy Freight locomotive

This locomotive used a 2-8-0 wheel configuration and was designed for heavy freight work. Such trains were a development of the earlier 2800 class.

They differed slightly from the earlier engines in several ways, most obviously because of the updated Collett side window cab. They were also built with external steam pipes. Between 1938 and 1941, 83 similar locomotives were built, although those made during World War Two did not have side window cabs, and some were plated over. This was a precaution against possible enemy air attack.

These locomotives were very popular with crews and drivers, and after nationalization in 1948 discussions were held with British Railways about building more. In the end, however, they were superseded by the BR Standard 9Fs. Engine number 3802, which was withdrawn in 1965, is now with the Llangollen Railway after restoration work.

GWR 823 Countess

Built in 1902 by Beyer Peacock & Co at their Gorton foundry in Manchester, the narrow gauge engine *Countess* still plies her trade on the Welshpool & Llanfair Railway. This particular railway was opened in 1903 to aid economic development in the area and was originally operated by Cambrian Railways. The line joined the former Oswestry & Newtown Railway station in Welshpool; to get there, it traversed difficult and twisty terrain, reaching a height of 600 feet. This required an engine design that was compact, sturdy and able to climb the steep gradients involved.

Countess is one of two of these engines at the railway and they were named after the Earl and Countess of Powis. Together, these locos ran the line from 1903 until it was closed in 1956.

The engines are much modified from when they were new, but are now in British Railways era colours, with *Countess* decked out in Great Western Livery. Cambrian Railways was absorbed by the Great Western Railway on 1 January 1922 as a result of the Railways Act of 1921.

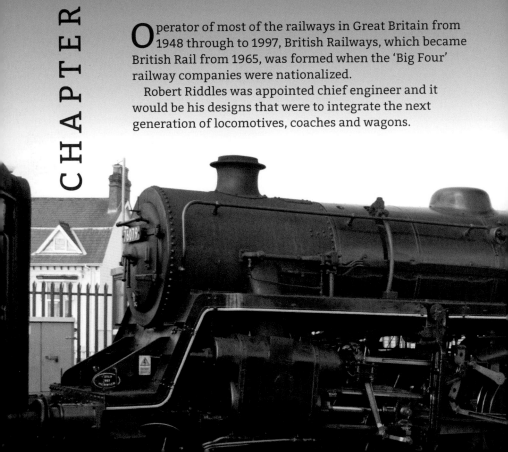

British Railways 1948

Operator of most of the railways in Great Britain from 1948 through to 1997, British Railways, which became British Rail from 1965, was formed when the 'Big Four' railway companies were nationalized.

Robert Riddles was appointed chief engineer and it would be his designs that were to integrate the next generation of locomotives, coaches and wagons.

The idea was to standardize all parts and fittings, creating easier maintenance across the whole range of locomotives.

During this time, there were also huge changes in the national railway network with the implementation of diesel locomotives and the electrification of lines. Steam locomotives were nearly all phased out by 1968 and replaced by diesel and electric power. Passenger revenue took precedence over freight, which was deserting the railways in favour of road transport, and one third of the network was closed down by the Beeching axe of the 1960s. The railways would never be the same again!

The British Rail logo, showing the 'double arrow', is made up of two interlocking arrows showing the direction of travel on a double-track railway. It was nicknamed 'the arrow of indecision'!

78019 British Railways Standard class 2

The British Railways Standard class 2 2-6-0 is one of BR's Standard classes of the 1950s. They were physically the smallest of the classes and 65 were built. No. 78019 was built at Darlington Works and was allocated to Kirkby Stephen where she worked on local and banking duties throughout the Lake District.

She then went to Willesden, Nuneaton and Crewe South. The locomotive was withdrawn in 1966 and sold to Woodham Brothers, Barry, moving there in 1967. The Severn Valley Railway rescued her in 1973 and stored her on a sideline. Following this, she was moved to Great Central Railway where she was restored.

These locomotives are often known by the nickname 'Mickey Mouse' and the entire fleet of 65 were built at Darlington Works. General consensus among the crews was that they were very sure-footed, although there were some complaints regarding the draughty and dirty footplate.

Locomotive number 80002 is a British Railways Standard class 4 2-6-4T tank engine built at Derby in 1952 from a design by R. A. Riddles. This locomotive is in preservation at the Keighley & Worth Railway and at the time of writing is awaiting an overhaul.

British Standard 4 locomotive

Designed by R. A. Riddles at the ex-LNER works at Doncaster, the British Railways Standard class 4 2-6-0 locomotives were built in three different places. Twenty-five were built at the works in Doncaster, while the remaining 90 of the 115-strong fleet were split between Horwick and the Derby Works – 76079 being built at the Horwick works. The last in the series, No. 76114, was also the last to be built at the 'Plant', as Doncaster Works was known.

The 5-foot, 3-inch-diameter driving wheels made the locomotive ideal for freight work and, with an axle loading of only 16 tons and 15 hundredweight, she was a very versatile engine with a route availablity that was virtually unrestricted. Batches were allocated to all British Railways regions, except Western.

76079

No. 76079 entered service with the London Midland region at Sutton Oak shed. She finished her days at Wigan (Springs Branch) in June 1967, before being towed to the Barry scrapyard in Wales behind the inevitable diesel engine.

In July 1974 she was moved to Steamport, Southport and became the 59th locomotive to be rescued from Barry. Engine number 76079 was the first locomotive to run from Wareham down to Corfe Castle and Swanage since 1967.

British Railways Standard class 5

The Standard class 5MT 4-6-0 built by British Railways in the 1950s was essentially a development of the LMS William Stanier Black Five, which is recognized as probably being the best mixed-traffic locomotive in Britain.

The design for the new locomotive was carried out at the ex-LNER Doncaster Works, the engine being fitted with all the latest ideas and overseen by R. A. Riddles, who was the chief mechanical engineer. While design took place at Doncaster, most of the actual assembly was carried out at the Derby Works.

No. 73096 was a Derby-built locomotive and was allocated the Patricroft shed, Manchester. She also worked at Shrewsbury, Gloucester and Nuneaton, before being withdrawn in 1967 and sent to Woodham Brothers' scrapyard in Wales. She was saved from demolition in 1985 and restoration was completed in October 1993.

The first of the class 73000 was introduced in April 1951 and by January of the following year there were already 30 in service. There was quite a gap before the next batch was assembled; Derby Works commenced building in

No. 73129 is a unique locomotive, being the only preserved Standard class 5 fitted with the Italian Capriotti valve-gear. She's another Derby Works locomotive, in fact the only survivor of the last batch of 30 made there in 1956. She was allocated to Shrewsbury in 1958 and then went to Patricroft, before being withdrawn in December 1967. She arrived in the Woodham Brothers' scrapyard in 1972, but was subsequently restored.

August 1955. A further 100 were then constructed up to 1957, with 42 being assembled at the Doncaster Works.

The first withdrawal took place on 29 February 1964, 73027 from the Swindon shed; and the last to be sent for scrap was 73069 from the Carnforth shed in August 1968.

Duke of Gloucester

The British Railways Standard class 8 4-6-2 Pacific steam locomotive number 71000 was designed by R. A. Riddles. The only one that was built was the prototype, which was named after the Duke of Gloucester and constructed at the Crewe Works in 1954.

The *Duke* as it is fondly known, was built to take the place of the Princess Royal class locomotive 46202, *Princess Anne*, which was involved in the Harrow and Wealdstone rail disaster of 1952.

The locomotive was based on the BR Standard class 7 Britannia design and was not popular with the crews due to poor steaming characteristics. Even trials undertaken by BR designed to improve performance left the locomotive and crews unhappy. Due to this, the *Duke* had a short working life of just eight years, before being withdrawn in 1962.

Initially destined for the National Collection, things moved on and only the cylinder arrangement proved to be of interest, so one of the cylinders was removed for display at the Science Museum. The other was removed to create a level balance before being scrapped. Apparently, it was sent to the wrong scrapyard at first, but when it did get to the Woodham Brothers' yard in Wales, it languished there for some time.

It was only saved from the scrapman by a group of enthusiasts in 1974, who rebuilt it as new in 13 years. Since then, alterations and modifications have been made to the engine, which turned it into one of the most powerful steam locomotives ever to run in Britain.

Black Prince

Designed by R. A. Riddles as the standard 'heavy freight' locomotive for British Railways, 92203 was one of 251 class 2-10-0s built at Swindon Works in January 1959. Although it carries the name *Black Prince*, it never used this name with British Railways.

The 9Fs were one of the most successful of the standard-class engines and ran very heavy freight trains at moderate speeds, and express passenger trains at speeds in excess of 80 mph. No. 92203 was working the heavy iron ore trains out of Bidston Dock, Birkenhead to Shotton Steel Works when it was taken out of service, after pulling the last steam-hauled ore train in November 1967.

BRUSH WITH FAME

In 1970 it formed part of the Longmoor Steam Railway and took part in a BBC TV documentary, *The Man Who Loves Giants*, which recounted the story of David Shepherd, who bought the engine. It also starred in *Young Winston*, a film about Winston Churchill growing up.

Following a boiler overhaul, it returned to service in 1979 and in 1982 it hauled the heaviest freight train – 2,198 tonnes – in Britain at Foster Yeoman's Tor Works.

The last days of steam

By the mid-1950s, it was clear that British Railways was in financial trouble, particularly its freight haulage business. More and more customers were sending their materials and goods via road or by aircraft, methods by which goods could be delivered to their final destination rather than somewhere nearby.

The government decided to order a review which was formally named the 'Modernization and Re-Equipment of the British Railways', or simply the 'Modernization Plan'. This report looked at bringing the railway system up to date. The UK had fallen behind many other countries regarding updating and modernizing its system, and now was the opportunity to change all that.

A White Paper was produced in 1954 which pointed out that modernization would eliminate the financial deficit of British Railways by 1962, and the recommendations were to increase speed, reliability, safety and line capacity, which was to be carried out by a series of measures that would make the system more attractive both to passengers and to freight operators.

The main areas briefly were:

'Electrification of principal main lines; large scale dieselization to replace steam locomotives; new passenger and freight and rolling stock; resignalling and track renewal; closure of a small number of lines, building of large freight marshalling yards.'

This was without doubt a huge undertaking, which many have since agreed was too much too quickly and badly organized. Orders for new diesels were overestimated and huge investment went into areas that were in complete decline, probably never to return to profit – road transport and containerization were taking over. New diesel

Crossing Scottish Highlands landscape is locomotive No 62005, a Peppercorn class K1 2-6-0 LNER engine built in 1949 and once called Lord of the Isles.

locomotives were also being rushed into service with little testing, resulting in poor build quality and reliability. Many areas even held on to their steam locomotives, which on occasion turned out to be more reliable than the diesels. New steam engines that had been planned prior to the 'Plan' were used for only a matter of a few years before being scrapped.

Major steam engine withdrawals happened from 1962 to 1966, with steam traction finally ending in August 1968. Many of the engines went on to be scrapped at various places around the UK, but probably the best known was Woodham Brothers, Barry in Wales, where hundreds of locomotives lay quietly rotting. The lucky ones were saved and many are now

Locomotive No. 30035, an M7 tank, based at Swanage, with Corfe Castle in the background.

running on our preserved lines, thanks to volunteers and those who are able to buy or organize associations that can look after and run these beautiful steaming giants.

BR Standard class 2 tank 41312 performed the last steam service on the Lymington branch in April 1967. The last three months of her career were spent at Nine Elms acting as a station shunter for Waterloo. She was finally withdrawn from service on 3 July 1967.

Now in semi-retirement, No. 41312 displays a proud notice which says:
'Last Day of Steam – 1 July 1858 to 2 April 1967
Brockenhurst to Lymington – last steam hauled branch on British Railways.'

The future brought diesel and diesel-electric locomotives and today we have trains that can run at more than 200 miles per hour. But is the UK railway system in better shape than in 1968; have we moved forward, or is it a case of everything has to change so that everything can remain the same?!

21C121 Dartmoor 34021

A West Country class locomotive, *Dartmoor* (see opposite) was built at the Brighton Works and started her working life in January of 1946. After a rebuild in 1957, she spent ten years working and was then withdrawn, having had a very short lifespan.

Above and below: These pictures of Dartmoor were taken at the Bluebell Railway steam day in 2007, where Eddystone, locomotive 34028, took the guise of Dartmoor to commemorate the 40th anniversary of the end of steam on Southern Rail on 9 July 1967. Dartmoor was one of the locomotives to operate on the last day, hauling a boat train from Southampton docks to Waterloo station, London.

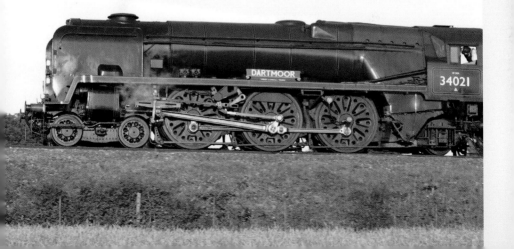

Industrial Locos

These hard-working little machines are often forgotten, simply because they barely figured in the public eye, but these little workhorses contributed so much to the industrial world of steam trains. Working behind the scenes in yards and depots, they toiled tirelessly, shunting and delivering just about anything from coal to coaches, around power stations or just in sidings.

These locomotives were with us from the very start and they were some of the very last to be withdrawn, some even continuing beyond the end of steam. Manufacturers such as Manning Wardle, Andrew Barclay, Hunslet, Robert Heath and of course Robert Stephenson, all designed and manufactured these amazing locomotives.

Many have been saved for preservation and it is great to see them in action once again, loved and looked after by their new owners.

Renishaw

Renishaw Ironworks No.6, 0-6-0ST locomotive was built in 1919 by Hudswell, Clarke and Company Limited, which was an engineering and locomotive building company in Jack Lane, Hunslet, Leeds.

Renishaw is based at the Tanfield Railway, the oldest railway in the world. It is currently at the Marley Hill engine shed going through a ten-year overhaul, but prior to that it was a regular on the line and no doubt will be again when it returns.

Meaford No. 2

This is *Meaford* No 2, a Robert Stephenson and Hawthorn 0-6-0 tank engine built in 1951 for British Electricity Authority Midlands Division. These big tank engines, of which there were 12 in the West Midlands alone, worked at the larger power stations in the UK.

Engine numbers 7683 and 7684 were built at the Forth Bank Works, Newcastle upon Tyne and then delivered to the Meaford Power Station, Barlaston in 1951, where they became *Meaford* No. 1 and No. 2. Later that year *Meaford* No. 2 was moved to Nechelles Power Station in Warwickshire and was renumbered *Meaford* No. 4. It spent the rest of its working life here until it was withdrawn.

Initially moved to the Battlefield Line Railway at Shackerstone in 1973 and restored to working order in 1995, it was moved to Foxfield in 1996, where it was given its original Meaford livery and title – *Meaford* No. 2.

Maid Marian

Maid Marian is a 0-4-0 saddle tank steam locomotive and was built in 1903 by the Hunslet Engine Company based in Leeds. She is currently based at the Bala Lake Railway in North Wales. The engine, works number 822 and subsequently named after a racehorse, spent her entire industrial life working at the Dinorwic Slate Quarry in North Wales.

She was purchased by a group of rail enthusiasts – the Maid Marian Locomotive Fund – in 1965 and they took possession of the engine in 1967.

Between 1967 and 1971, Maid Marian could be seen at the Bressingham Steam Museum, after which she went to the Llanberis Lake Railway. In 1975 she resumed working life at the Bala Lake Railway.

Lewisham

Lewisham is named after Viscount Lewisham, chairman of the Shropshire Beet Sugar Company at Alscott, where the engine was delivered from new. She is a 0-6-0 saddle tank locomotive and was built by W. G. Bagnall in 1927 at their Castle Works in Stafford.

Lewisham was replaced by a diesel loco and British Sugar, who bought out the SBS Company, were talking about placing her on a plinth in Shrewsbury, but eventually she was given to Foxfield Light Railway, finding her way there in 1970. Over the years, she has presented herself in several guises, including the blue-lettered 'British Sugar'; currently she's in unlined green.

Asbestos

When new, *Asbestos* was delivered to her owners, Washington Chemical Company, County Durham, which in 1920 became a subsidiary of the Turner and Newall Company Ltd. She worked there until 1933 when she transferred to Turner and Newall, Trafford Park Works, Manchester. Here, they made asbestos and that is where her name came from. The engine was donated by the company to Chasewater Railway in 1968.

The loco is a Hawthorn, Leslie 0-4-0ST, 2780 of 1909 and was built at the company's Forth Bank Works, Newcastle-upon-Tyne.

Above: Asbestos *is seen double-heading with Bagnall 0-4-0, 15-inch, four-coupled saddle tank engine 2623* Hawarden, *built in 1940. Bagnall was founded in 1875 by William Gordon Bagnall and based at the Castle Engine Works in Castle Town in Stafford.*

Left: Asbestos *came to the Chasewater Railway in 1968 and not long after became the first locomotive to steam on the railway. This locomotive was built by R&W Hawthorn Leslie and Company Limited – generally known as Hawthorn Leslie. The company was a shipbuilder and locomotive manufacturer and was based in Newcastle upon Tyne.*

National Coal Board No. 6

Described on their own site as one of the unique gems of the steam collection at Foxfield, this Robert Heath 0-4-0 saddle tank was built in 1885 and rebuilt in 1934; No. 6 is a thoroughly local engine and a very remarkable survivor.

Robert Heath & Sons were well known local ironmasters, at one time reputed to be the largest producers of bar iron in the world. Furnaces, forges and mills were operated at Black Bull, Biddulph and Ford Green, together with collieries and a network of private railway lines.

It seems that the company, having bought a new locomotive from Falcon of Loughborough, decided that they would make a copy of her; the first of which became No. 6. Eleven more four-wheeled

locomotives were built up to World War One and two larger locomotives were also built post-war, again copies of engines purchased in 1888 from Black Hawthorn.

After spending her working life at the Black Bull and Norton collieries, No. 6 was sent to the Cowlishaw Walker workshops in 1934 for a rebuild. In 1947 when the National Coal Board was established, No. 6 continued to work at the Norton colliery, while many of her contemporaries were decommissioned.

No. 6 was the first one to be built by Heaths and the only one to survive. As can be imagined, externally she was not in good condition, but Staffordshire County Council Museum took an interest in purchasing the engine as part of a collection of railway relics for a proposed museum at Shugborough Hall. The NCB kindly donated the engine in 1969, but the museum never happened and No. 6 was moved to the Chatterley Whitfield Mining Museum in 1983. A group of members from Foxfield, determined that No. 6 should stay in the area, organized the purchase and in 1994 she was moved to the Foxfield Railway. After 120 years of life – after a further overhaul and plenty of TLC – she is still keeping herself busy.

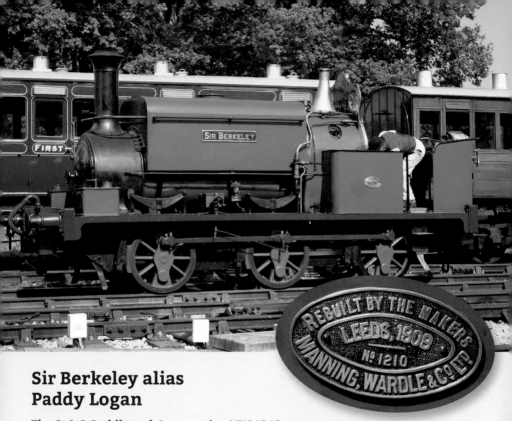

Sir Berkeley alias Paddy Logan

The 0-6-0 Saddletank Locomotive MW 1210 was
built in 1890 by Manning Wardle & Co. at their Boyne Engine Works in
Leeds. It was delivered as new to the engineering contractors Logan &
Hemingway and allocated the number 30. Initially put to work building
the Manchester, Sheffield & Lincolnshire Railway (later the Great Central
Railway), it moved on to the excavation of the Nottingham GCR/GNR joint
station site (Nottingham Victoria).

Following a slack period, the locomotive was renumbered 10 and
continued working on railway-related construction. In 1935 Logan &

Hemingway went into liquidation and it was sold to the Cranford Ironstone Company of Kettering. It was here that it received the nameplate *Sir Berkeley*, which came from a scrapped Manning Wardle engine. It seems though that, to the Cranford workforce, it was always known as *Paddy Logan*.

The engine was made redundant in 1957 and formally retired in 1963, after which it was saved from the scrap man and bought in 1964. It was taken to the Worth Valley Railway.

Sir Berkeley's ten-year boiler certification expired in 2001. A new boiler was built in 2006 and *Sir Berkeley* returned to service at the Middleton Railway, Leeds on Saturday 14 April 2007.

BRUSH WITH FAME

In 1968 it took part in the BBC Television production of *The Railway Children*.

Wimblebury

This beautiful-looking engine goes by the name of *Wimblebury*.
She was built by Hunslet of Leeds in 1956 and delivered to the
National Coal Board, Cannock Wood Colliery near Hednesford
in Staffordshire that same year. She is an Austerity class, 0-6-0
saddle tank and has the number 3839.

She worked at Cannock Wood Colliery until she was
withdrawn in 1970, when she was destined to be used for spares
for another loco. *Wimblebury* was bought for preservation and
moved to Foxfield in 1973, where, after work had been carried
out, she was regularly seen pulling trains in the mid-1970s.

Stagshaw

Locomotive 0-6-0ST *Stagshaw* was built
by Hawthorn Leslie in 1923 and should
have been an example of a Cristiani
compressed-steam-system locomotive
(a railway locomotive with a piston

engine which could run on either steam from a boiler or diesel fuel). However, this didn't work, and so *Stagshaw* was converted to a conventional steam locomotive and is currently stored at Tanfield Railway, a standard gauge heritage railway in Gateshead and County Durham.

Edward Thomas

Edward Thomas is a narrow gauge steam locomotive built by Kerr Stuart & Co. Ltd., at their California Works in Stoke-on-Trent in 1921. It was delivered to the Corris Railway where it worked until 1948.

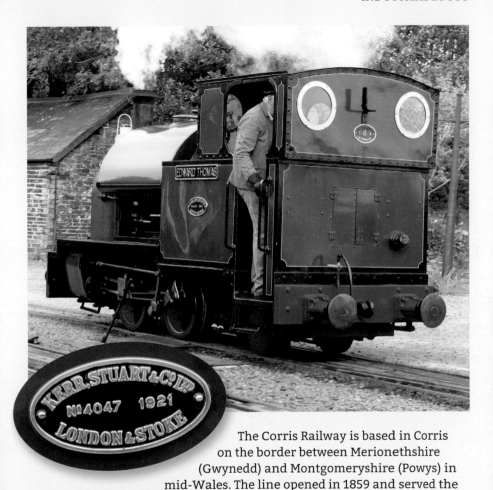

The Corris Railway is based in Corris on the border between Merionethshire (Gwynedd) and Montgomeryshire (Powys) in mid-Wales. The line opened in 1859 and served the slate quarries at Corris Uchaf, Aberllefenni, the isolated quarries around Ratgoed and quarries along the length of the Dulas Valley.

Edward Thomas, engine number 4, closely followed by another engine based at the Talyllyn Railway, engine number 2 *Dolgoch*. *Edward Thomas* was purchased by the railway in 1951 and was named after the former manager of the railway. Until 2000 the engine was running under the guise of *Peter Sam* and in red livery. There was a change of colour scheme to British Railways black and then after an overhaul in 2004, 'she' returned to service on Sunday 30 May as *Edward Thomas*, in unlined green livery. A final change came and the train took on the standard Talyllyn Railway livery of deep bronze lined with black borders and yellow lining.

Dolgoch, a narrow gauge 0-4-0 well tank steam locomotive, was built by Fletcher, Jennings & Co. in 1866 and is one of the oldest locomotives still in active service. She went to the Talyllyn Railway in 1866 and is still there. Between 1900 and 1914, the engine was renamed Pretoria, after the relief of that township in South Africa during the Boer War. After regaining the name *Dolgoch*, she has resisted any alteration ever since.

Douglas

Built in 1918 by Andrew Barclay & Co Ltd., *Douglas* is a narrow gauge steam locomotive. Initially used by the Air Service Constructional Corp (Royal Air Force), Douglas spent most of its working life at RAF Calshot near Southampton. In 1949 it was bought by the engineering company Abelson & Co. Ltd, before being given to the Talyllyn Railway in 1953, who named the engine after the donor Douglas Abelson.

BRUSH WITH FAME

All the steam-operated engines on the Talyllyn Railway have appeared in 'The Railway Series' books by the Rev. W. Awdry on the Skarloey Railway. *Douglas* plays the part of *Duncan*, who apparently is a stubborn engine that likes to complain that he is overworked. He is also known for swaying on the track dangerously, which his driver calls 'Rock 'n' Roll'. *Duncan* first appeared in season 4 of the TV series, and reappears frequently.

Alice

The steam locomotive known as *Alice* is a Hunslet
0-4-0ST and used to work in the Dinorwic slate
quarries at Llanberis, in North Wales. She was built
in 1902, as Works No. 780 and originally known as No. 4.

Between 1886 and 1932, 15 similar engines were supplied, the first of which was *Velinheli*, Works No. 409, but for some reason the class was named after the first *Alice*. Like most of her class, *Alice* did not have a dome, but a steam chamber produced by the firebox outer shell being raised some six inches above the boiler barrel. Cabs were not regularly fitted in those days since these engines would have to proceed under low bridges and through tunnels in the quarries.

The Dinorwic slate quarry was where *Alice* spent most of her working life, but by the early 1960s she could be found partially dismantled for spares in the Australia Gallery.

Alice finally had all her parts returned to her and, after much toing and froing, she was restored and, though she visited many different railways, she finally ended up at the Bala Lake Railway, North Wales.

A variety of LNER goods locomotives parked in sidings after loading up with water and coal. Photographed in 1930, this was a typical scene of the period during the heyday of the steam train.

Picture Credits

The majority of pictures were supplied by the author.

Thanks also go to:
Science & Society Picture Library – 12BL (NRM/Pictorial Collection), 18L (Science Museum), 80T (National Railway Museum)
Getty Images – 223–4 (Fox Photos)
Mary Evans Picture Library – 9 (Thaliastock), 20 (The Institute of Mechanical Engineers)
Milepost 92 ½ Picture Library – 52-3, 72, 105, 131
Shutterstock – 10, 26
Cover image: Getty Images

The author would like to thank all the many preserved railways, their informative websites and their personnel, who gladly helped with information and who voluntarily give their time to keep our fond memories alive. Thanks also to the owners of these grand smoking giants, who take pride in allowing us to see and experience the way life once used to be when steam was not just a dream.

Due to the nature of the subject, much of the research was carried out from many different sources, both on the World Wide Web and in local libraries. I would like to thank all these sources, of which there are too many to mention, but they are well known to locomotive enthusiasts.

• Please note that due to the age and often inconsistent information, some figures given in this book may be subject to discussion. Wherever possible we have attempted to give the correct information, but we apologize for any statement that may be misleading or incorrect.